Following

JESUS

IN THE FOOTSTEPS

of

FRANCIS

FR. JOHN ANGLIN, OFM

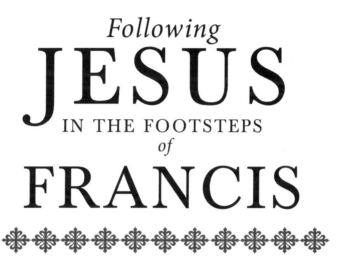

Following
JESUS
IN THE FOOTSTEPS
of
FRANCIS

A Guide to Living a Franciscan Spirituality For Everyone

Lantern Books ● New York
A Division of Booklight Inc.

2017
Lantern Books
128 Second Place
Brooklyn, NY 11231
www.lanternbooks.com

Dedicated to the many friars, sisters,
Secular Franciscans, and friends with a
Franciscan heart who have shaped my life

Acknowledgements

IT SHOULD BE obvious that in writing a book on the subject of Franciscan spirituality that I am extremely grateful to all of the friars who inspired my Franciscan vocation back when I was a student at Columbus High School in Boston as well as all of the friars, Franciscan sisters, and Secular Franciscans that have been part of my life over the past fifty-one years. Not only have I learned from their teaching, I have also been inspired by many of them to become a better Franciscan.

I would particularly like to thank my brothers—Roderic Petrie, OFM, and Daniel Lanahan, OFM—for the "intervention" they did with me in January of 2011. At that time, I had preached a retreat to the friars using many of the themes presented in this book. After one of the retreat conferences, they pulled me aside and said, "John, this is an intervention." I was puzzled. After all, that term is generally used to confront a person who has a drug or alcohol problem.

Seeing my puzzled look, they then told me, "John, you just have to write a book." That got me going, and I wrote *The Wandering Friar*, which was published in 2013. I loved writing that book, and it has been well received, but I knew that I was not really fulfilling the terms of that intervention until I wrote on Franciscan spirituality. This book seals the deal on that. Thanks very much, Dan and Rod, for starting my engine as a writer. I want to thank Dan and Rod as well as Anthony Carrozzo, OFM, for taking the time to read through this work and offer me suggestions for its improvement.

I most especially want to thank the friars of Holy Name Province who have been supportive of my attempts at writing, and above all, the other friars here at St. Anthony Friary. There are many lay people, some of them close friends and some of them people I met in passing during parish missions, who have encouraged me to write. To all of them, a big thanks!

Contents

Introduction

"Everybody loves the friars." These are words that I have often heard spoken during my more than fifty years of living the Franciscan life. Though at times I wonder if we deserve to be loved, that is not the point. The fact is that there is something about us that people love, something that draws them to us. I experienced that "something" as a youngster when I was drawn to attend a high school staffed by the friars and a few years later when I decided to become one. Just what is that something? At the age of seventeen when I decided to enter the order, I could not put words to the answer for that question. I just felt it and was drawn to it. I now believe that the something was and is Franciscan spirituality lived by those friars that I first met those many years ago. I didn't think of it right away as spirituality and neither do most folks who love the Franciscans. People say things like "They're real," "They're down to earth," "They relate to ordinary people," and

"They understand our struggles." These are the kind of things that made me want to be a friar. All of these are true when we Franciscans are living our lives as we should, and they are the by-products of what I call Franciscan spirituality, a unique way of relating to God and to others that brings out those qualities. It is, by the way, the spirituality and approach to ministry in the Church that is being called forth by Pope Francis, our Jesuit pope with a Franciscan heart. I believe that from the moment he stepped out on the balcony in Rome to give his first blessing as pope, people embraced him because he reflected, as a Jesuit, these Franciscan qualities.

In this book, I would like to put forth what I believe are the essential elements of that spirituality in a way that everyone—friars, sisters, diocesan priests, and lay people alike can apply to their lives. In fact, if you are seeking and searching, not sure if you can believe in God, or Jesus, or the Church, I invite you to be open to what is offered here. We friars do not have a monopoly on living that spirituality. In fact, St. Francis did not originally set out to form a religious order. He intended first of all to follow Jesus and live the Gospel and to show everyone that they could do that too, even the simplest and most unlettered peasants of his time, even the poorest and simplest folks of our own times as well. The first Franciscans were lay people. It was only a few years later when some other men from Assisi wanted to join with Francis that a formal *order* began to emerge.

Over the eight centuries since the Franciscan movement first began (early thirteenth century), our way of life has been lived by friars, Poor Clare Nuns, Franciscan Sisters, members of the Secular Franciscan Order (once called the Third Order), and many others not formally affiliated to an organized Franciscan community. My recently deceased confrere Fr. Roy Gasnick, OFM, in his work, *The Francis Book*, called this latter group the Fourth Order.[1]

What I hope to set forth here is not some sort of spiritual roadmap that will take you from point A to B to C, etc., but rather to spell out some of the essential elements that going into living a Franciscan life whether it be lived in a friary or convent or the kitchen or a factory.

Another popular saying about the friars is, "If you've seen one Franciscan, you've seen one Franciscan." In other words, there is no Franciscan mold; rather, in each one, there is a unique way of living out the elements that are spoken of in this book. In addition to that as the journey of life goes on, each one revisits these various aspects of our life, renews our commitment to them, or perhaps pays attention to some aspect of it all that we have forgotten. This entire sentiment was expressed by Francis himself as he was dying in words related to us by St. Bonaventure in his *Major Legend of Saint Francis*, "I have done what is mine; may Christ teach you what is yours."[2] I believe that he could say this because the life he had set out to live and had invited others to share with him was basically a life of living the Gospel. That task is so challenging but also so basic that it can be lived out in any number of ways.

So whether you are a seasoned veteran of Franciscan life or someone who is just starting out on the journey, I pray that this book will be a useful and helpful companion for you.

Spirituality and Religion

BEFORE PROCEEDING WITH my presentation of Franciscan spirituality, I would like to describe more clearly what I think spirituality is and how it interfaces with religion, how the two go together. Though I argued with myself over the necessity of including this chapter, I decided that the issue it addresses is an important one in today's religious climate and needs to be dealt with by anyone writing on the subject of spirituality.

I have heard many people in recent years make the statement, "I'm spiritual but not religious." I believe that this way of looking at things has its origins in the followers of Alcoholics Anonymous (AA) and other twelve-step programs. These are wonderful programs, and I myself have participated in the AL-Anon program for people affected by alcoholism. The twelve steps call on people to surrender to a higher power in order to let go of their addictions, codependencies, etc. They basically say that you have to be open to someone or something bigger than yourself to overcome your problem. It is this openness and even surrender to a higher power that makes these programs spiritual. That act of surrender, in fact, is the essence of spirituality. The twelve-step programs are not opposed to religion. They just don't want religious difference to get in the way of dealing with one's problem. That is all well and good, but what has evolved out of that distinction between spirituality and religion is a belief by some that you can't be both spiritual and religious at the same time, that there is an incompatibility between the two. There are many reasons for this, but probably the greatest is disillusionment with organized religion, especially among younger people, and even among those who identify themselves as Christian. A recent survey conducted by the Pew Forum on Religion and Public Life states that nearly 20% of Americans are not affiliated with any religion, and the number is over 30% for those under 30.[3] If we add to that the many who claim to belong to a church but who still claim to be more spiritual than religious, the numbers climb significantly.

What can be done to address this issue? It would be easy to blame the various churches and their leaders as well as ordinary members, and, to be sure, a great deal of blame can be laid there. On the other hand, I think that we need to challenge those who make this statement. Is it not easier to be your own spiritual guide and to follow a path that makes you comfortable rather than listening to someone who presents you with a challenging belief? Is it not easier as well to hang around with like-minded people or to walk away from religion because some of its adherents are phony or because some have engaged in scandalous behavior? One of the earliest heresies in Christian history was Gnosticism, which boils down to its simplest term as a belief that salvation was only open to the truly pure and enlightened?

Another dimension of this problem comes from the fact that even when churches have the best of leaders, issues of family life often come into play and lead to an alienation from religion. All too often dysfunctional and/or abusive parents rigidly impose an unhealthy form of religion on their children, and as the children become adults, they understandably run from religion.

Let's take a look then at spirituality and religion and see where they complement each other. Fr. Ronald Rolheiser, OMI, one of my favorite spiritual writers, defines spirituality as "what we do with our desire."[4] He goes on to say that "it [desire] takes its root in the *eros* inside of us and it's all about how we shape and discipline that *eros*."[5] Some explanation is in order here. Father Rolheiser is using the word *eros* in the deepest and truest sense of the word. It is not to be confused with our modern sexualized understanding of the word but rather as the driving force in all of us that propels us toward our deepest longings and union with others and with God. Eros, of course, can include sexual desire, which can be something beautiful or something destructive. He uses three examples of people that he believes were very spiritual, one of them a truly holy woman, one a good but flawed woman, one a tragically self-destructive woman. The three women are Mother Teresa, Princess Diana, and Janice Joplin. I think that you can figure out which category fits each one. All of them had, in his opinion, strong spiritual energy but developed, or not, in different ways. I believe that this understanding of spirituality is what St. Augustine had in mind when he wrote, "To praise you is the desire of a man, a little piece of your creation. You stir man to take pleasure in praising you, because you have made us for yourself, and our heart is restless until it rests in you."[6]

For our purposes, let us say that spirituality is the process of directing our deepest longings and yearnings toward God and, in that process, growing ever closer to God and finally surrendering to God. When that happens, our desire becomes a prayer. As Christians, that relationship with God is directed toward Jesus, the Son of God, and is guided by the Holy Spirit working in us. That works for those of us who are believers but can we speak of a secular spirituality? There are, indeed, agnostics and atheists who consider themselves to be spiritual. Insofar as they shape and discipline their eros (desire) toward a higher goal, such as making a better world, I think we can accept them at their word even if we who believe think that there is something lacking in that. Yes, you can be spiritual without being religious. The issue, however, is "Can the two go together?"

To answer that question, we need to ask, "What then is religion?" The Merriam-Webster dictionary defines it as "a personal or institutional system of religious attitudes, beliefs, and practices."[7] I believe this to be a good working definition of religion that can be applied to Christianity, Judaism, Hinduism, Buddhism, Islam, or any other religion. What all religions in some way have in common is that they began with some sort of spiritual experience. Abraham and Moses had deep and meaningful encounters with God that shaped Judaism. Jesus himself, at his baptism in the Jordan, experienced his deep relationship with the Father and the Spirit. The apostles in their encounters with the Risen Christ had the foundational experience in Christianity. That is why we always refer to the Church as founded on the faith of the apostles. The founders of other religions also had deep, spiritual experiences that shaped their particular religion.

How then did religion and spirituality become separated? For the founding members of a faith, their spiritual experience, their encounter with God, led them to rituals, beliefs, and moral codes that gave expression to their original spiritual experience. In some cases, God revealed to them that such practices and beliefs be followed. For these founders, the original spiritual experience or encounter with God was transformative. It changed their lives. As large numbers of adherents began to follow a particular religion, there were those who observed all of the rituals and moral codes but who did not have a deep experience of God in the process.

Following the rules became an end in itself rather than a means of drawing closer to God. For many, the observation of rules and the keeping of rituals becomes a reward system—do this and you will go to heaven. Staying with the Catholic experience, what happens is that many people try to keep all the rules and observe all the practices, but it becomes routine. When this happens, some people keep practicing the faith out of duty or obligation but without experiencing a closer encounter with God while others feel bored and wonder what it all means. These folks usually fall away from the practice of the faith, or they live the faith with a rigid and legalistic approach.

Because of this every religion periodically experiences the need for reform. This can be a tricky issue. Reform only of externals does not necessarily lead to spiritual growth. The reforms in the Catholic Church after the Second Vatican Council were meant to draw people closer to God, to Christ by doing things like allowing the Mass and the Sacraments to be celebrated in the vernacular languages and relaxing some of the stricter rules that accompanied the living of the faith. Indeed there was a true spiritual renewal that took place. Many Catholics spoke of encountering Jesus more closely, reading and meditating on the Scriptures, etc. Spiritual renewal movements like the Cursillo, Marriage Encounter, and the Charismatic renewal were genuine sources of spiritual growth for many. In local parishes, there was a renewed sense of vitality. At the same time for many people, there developed a spirit of change for the sack of change of "Out with the old and in with the new." As a result of this, many genuine sources of prayer and renewal fell by the wayside and many experiments with liturgy and prayer were mundane expressions of triviality.

What then is the key to bringing religion and spirituality together? Quite simply the answer is surrender that leads to transformation. This is at the heart of the twelve-step programs and is expressed in the third step—"Turned our will and our lives over to the care of God as we understood Him."[8] Many people adhere to religious practice and custom but never surrender, never really turn their lives over to God. From a Christian perspective, it is so easy to forget that Jesus does not call us to keep rules but to follow Him by taking up the cross every day and following Him (see Lk. 9:23–24). To the extent that the Christian does that, he or she is transformed and becomes more and more like Christ. St. Paul expresses this beautifully in the letter to the Galatians when he says, "I live, no longer I, but Christ lives in me" (Gal. 2:20).

As Catholics, to the extent that we surrender our lives to Christ whom we meet in the Eucharist, in the wider sacramental life of the Church, in God's Word as well is in the poor of this world (see Mt. 25), we are living a spiritual and religious life. I would go so far as to say that keeping all the rules and customs without such surrender, without growing in union with Christ, without therefore being spiritual is to miss the point entirely. It is the unhealthy and superficial practice of religion that falsely leads too many people into the path of being spiritual but not religious. Healthy religion is always deeply spiritual. The two need not be separated.

Jesus Himself was aware of this very problem. Throughout the Gospels, we find him addressing this issue. The parable of the Pharisee and the Tax collector in Luke 18:9–14 is a fine illustration of this. The Pharisee recites all of his good deeds and observance of the rule to justify himself. The tax collector opens himself to Jesus and admits his sinfulness. Jesus tells us that the tax collector, not the Pharisee, went home justified. His justification comes in admitting his need for help and forgiveness and in admitting that he can't justify himself by his own good deeds.

Now that we have looked at the interface of spirituality and religion and given a broad definition of what Catholic Christian spirituality entails, we can move on to a look at Franciscan spirituality.

Franciscan Spirituality

Telling the Story

TRYING TO LAY out in a book like this the essence of what constitutes Franciscan spirituality can be quite a challenge. You see, unlike what St. Ignatius of Loyola did for the Jesuits, there is no set of "exercises," those steps that lead us from one theme to another along the spiritual journey. Likewise, there are no descriptions of stages of spiritual growth and images like "interior castles," or the "Dark night of the Soul" such as we find in Teresa of Avila and her fine presentation of Carmelite spirituality. For us Franciscans, there is no brief compendium or workbook to follow.

What then are the sources of our spirituality? Where do we look for guidance in this area? In English, anyway, we have the 1972 *Omnibus of Sources* published by the Franciscan Herald Press and later the three-volume series entitled

Francis of Assisi: Early Documents published by the Franciscan Institute of St. Bonaventure University through New City Press in 1999, 2000, and 2001. I will, by the way, use this latter series in quoting the early Franciscan sources. We do not find in these volumes any organized schema to set us out on our spiritual journey. What we do find are the very brief writings of St. Francis, including the two rules for Franciscan life that he wrote as well as some prayers and letters of exhortation to different groups. We also find there his *Admonitions*, wise and sage bits of spiritual advice given at various points in his life. Beyond that, there are pages and pages of stories, stories that include biographies of Francis written from different points of view by the early members of the order, and stories of the various early friars that include both their heroic living of saintly and virtuous lives as well as their many foibles and shortcomings.

What are we to make of this for our own spiritual journeys? I believe that the answer to this question is simply this—we look to the stories of Francis and the early members of the order, stories of how they encountered Christ and drew closer to him, as well as stories of how they fell short of the mark, in order to better tell our own spiritual stories to see and understand how the Christ story is continually being told in the stories of each one of us who seek to follow Jesus in the footsteps of Francis of Assisi. We likewise, through the living of community life, see how the Christ story is relived in our brothers and sisters and in ourselves today. In this sense, we can say that Franciscan spirituality is a "story spirituality,"[1] a spirituality which challenges us each in our own unique way to allow our lives to be more and more conformed to Christ, to allow His story and our story to merge together yet in a unique way in each one of us. This is true whether one is a Friar Minor, a Poor Clare, a Third Order religious, a Secular Franciscan, or an ordinary person not formally affiliated with the order who is striving to follow Christ in a Franciscan way.

To understand this approach we can look to two sayings attributed to St. Francis. In the first one, cited in a 1318 set of writings called *The Mirror of Perfection*, he tells us:

> That a good Lesser Brother is one who would possess the life and qualities of the following holy brothers: namely, the faith and love of poverty which Brother Bernard most perfectly had; the simplicity and purity of Brother Leo who was truly a man of most holy purity; the courtly bearing of Brother Angelo who was the first soldier to enter the Order and was endowed with every courtesy and kindness; the friendly manner and common sense of Brother Masseo, together with his attractive and gracious eloquence; the mind raised in contemplation which Brother Giles has even to the highest perfection; the virtuous and constant prayer of Brother Rufino who, whatever he was doing, even sleeping, always prayed without ceasing and whose mind was always intent on the Lord; the patience of Brother Juniper, who achieved the perfect state of patience because he always kept in mind the perfect

truth of his low estate and the ardent desire to imitate Christ through the way of the cross; the bodily and spiritual strength of Brother John of Lauds, who at the time in his robust body surpassed everyone; the charity of Brother Roger whose life and conduct were spent in ardent love; the solicitude of Brother Lucidus who had the greatest care and concern and did not want to remain in any place for a month, and when he enjoyed staying in some place, would immediately leave, saying: "We do not have a dwelling place here on earth, but in Heaven."[2]

The same point is expressed more succinctly in the previous quoted words of Francis found in St. Bonaventure's work on the life of Francis, "I have done what is mine, may Christ teach you yours."[3]

So whether you live in a friary or convent or in an ordinary home, if you are trying to allow Christ to live in you in your own unique way and you are open to how he is living just as truly but differently in others, you are living this dimension of Franciscan spirituality.

Part 1:
The Theological Vision Behind Franciscan Spirituality

WHY A PARTICULAR Franciscan spirituality, or Jesuit, or Carmelite, etcetera? Aren't all Christians simply called to follow Jesus? The answer to the last question is obviously yes. The mystery of Christ, however, is so deep and meaningful that different people feel inclined to emphasize different aspects of the Christian journey without, of course, excluding anything that is essential. This is true not only with spiritualities developed within the traditions of various religious orders but also those developed within various lay movements and societies within the Church. Pax Christi, the Cursillo movement, the Charismatic Renewal, the Marriage Encounter and many others are examples of this. They are all legitimately Christian and Catholic but are likewise very different ways of following Christ. While it's beyond the scope of this book to delve into other churches, I'm sure we can speak of Baptist, Episcopal, Lutheran, Presbyterian, and Methodist, spiritualities as well.

In this section, I wish to draw attention to the teachings of the Scriptures and the Church that Franciscans, beginning with Francis himself, emphasized in living out their spiritual journey. With Francis, we cannot claim that he had an organized theology. He rather had a life experience of God. Later, theologians from the order, most notably St. Bonaventure and Blessed John Duns Scotus, reflected on that experience and developed theological approaches that have guided Franciscans now for several centuries.

I do not attempt to set forth an in-depth look at these teachings but rather to present a summary of Franciscan thought to assist the ordinary reader in acquiring a basic understanding of these various theological trends. I would also remind the reader that theological ideas and expressions do not make anyone a spiritual person, but they do shape the way in which one's spirituality develops.

For those who wish to delve further and take an in-depth look at these ideas, I have tried to reference everything that I say and have likewise provided a bibliography at the end of this book.

Who Are You, O God?
Who am I?

THE TWO QUESTIONS in title of this chapter are taken from words that Francis is reported to have spoken in prayer, words overheard by his close companion, Brother Leo, while he was in prayer during a forty-day retreat that lead up to Francis receiving the gift of the *stigmata* (the imprinting of the wounds of Jesus on his hands, feet, and side).[1] Francis never wrote a treatise on God. He was not a theologian. His writings and, above all, the prayers that he composed reflect several things about his experience of God. I will refer to two of them here and one other in the next chapter. The first is that God was transcendent. He never used that fancy word but rather spoke of the Most High and Glorious God in the prayers that he used. For example, in his Praises of God prayer, he says, "You are strong. You are great. You are the most high.

You are the almighty king. You Holy Father, King of heaven and earth."[2] How did he come to see God in this way? I believe that he beheld the beauty and vastness of creation and concluded that the God who created all of that must be beyond anything or anyone that we can understand. If one travels to Assisi and looks up to the town from the valley below, or if one looks down to the valley from the town itself, or even better from the peak of Monte Subasio on which Assisi rests, the view is breathtaking. I often wonder how Francis would react if he were to see the pictures taken by the Hubble telescope. If you have Internet access, you might check out the following sites: http://hubblesite.org/gallery/album/entire/ and www.slideshare.net/bpk_matrix/fantastic-trip-83039. I behold these pictures with awe and with the realization that God is not someone we can figure out. Yes, in faith we come to believe what we read in the Scriptures and what the Church teaches, but God as God is still so much more than we can imagine. Francis instinctively knew this. I find that many well-meaning people today can reflect a glib and simplistic view of God. Most are people who pray often and feel close to God. That is a good thing, but with it comes the temptation to think that God is almost our equal. We know better, of course, but I think that while we should not have a fear-based or punitive sense of God, we should maintain a sense of awe and reverence before God.

While Francis had a deep sense of the awesomeness of God, he also saw the beauty and goodness of God.

Unfortunately for many people, a mighty God, a powerful God, is not always a kind God. Not so for St. Francis and for us Franciscans. In the previously cited Praises of God prayer, Francis praises God for being charity, wisdom, humility, meekness, and goodness, and that is these are only a few of the many qualities for which he praises God. How does he come to this? Again, I refer to his contemplation of God's presence in nature, in creation. Quite simply for him, the God who created such goodness and beauty must be good and beautiful by nature. Also, there is the fact that because he experienced so much violence and evil in his days as a soldier, days which disillusioned him about warfare and fighting, he found in God exactly the opposite of what he experienced in those difficult years. Above all, however, it was in his ongoing contemplation of Jesus in His humanity, as we shall see in the next chapter, that he saw the greatest expression of God's goodness.

The second question in the title of this chapter is "Who am I?" In Francis's time, there were no psychologically based personality surveys to help one answer that question. Francis's answer is juxtaposed with the first question, "Who are you, O God?" In other words, he is reflecting on who he is in reference to the Almighty. Some of his answers to this question give the impression that he was being harsh on himself. For example, in the previously mentioned dialogue with Brother Leo, he says, "Who am I, a worm and your little servant."[3] What is he telling us here? It is true that like many great saints, he is often deeply aware of his sinfulness, but I think that his use of the word *worm* here has another connotation. He is saying that God is great and he is small. God is the Creator and he is the creature. He is not so much putting himself down as he is putting his life in perspective. Once again in the dialogue with Brother Leo, he says,

> I am totally yours, O Lord, and I have nothing except a tunic and a cord and trousers, and these are likewise yours. Therefore what can I offer to the greatness of your dominion? Heaven and earth, fire and water and everything that is in them are yours, O Lord.[4]

Interestingly, in "The Admonitions," a collection of various words of advice and counsel to the early friars, he writes, "What a person is before God, that he is and no more."[5] One final insight into Francis's answer to this question can be found by understanding the context of his beautiful poem entitled "Canticle of the Creatures." An initial reading of the canticle might suggest that the romantic and idealistic heart of the young Francis composed this work. Not so. It was composed later in his life when he was going blind and suffering in several other ways. He was taking a respite at San Damiano where the Poor Clares were residing. He was in a little shelter outside the convent building. Upon awakening one morning, he felt the warmth of the sun on him and composed the first part of the canticle to Brother Sun, Sister Moon, Brother Wind, and Sister Water. He was praising them as his brothers and sisters because they, like him, were creatures, not the Creator, and he joined them in praising God. We will take a deeper look at this canticle in a later chapter.

And what might we learn from these two questions posed by Francis to God? I suggest that we pray them for a while as a kind mantra and then try to answer them honestly. Who is God, for you and for me? The answer is not to be found in catechisms and works of theologians but rather in our own hearts based on our life experience as people of faith who have probably struggled at times, wondering who God really is, or why God hasn't answered a prayer. In the end, we hopefully realize that as for Francis, God is simply awesome beyond our wildest imagination.

And who am I? Am I my accomplishments, my college degrees, my money, or the items on my resume, or does my real identity lie in something deeper, in the fact that I too am a creature in the hands of the Creator, a child of God who is loved in a special and unique way?

The Big Wow

The Incarnation

THE THIRD AND most important quality of God in the life of Francis was humility. Because he experienced God as awesome and mighty, and at the same time good, he was, to use a modern phrase, bowled over by the fact that God, in humble love for us, became one of us and went to the cross out of love for us. I like to refer to this as Francis's "BIG WOW." It is certainly a big *wow* for me, and I hope it is also for those who are reading this book. Imitating this humility in our own lives, as we will see in a later chapter, is foundational for living a Franciscan way of life.

Right from the beginning of his spiritual journey, Francis was in awe of the goodness and humility of God in creating us and in doing so many wonderful things for us. His greatest expression of the gift of the Incarnation, of God taking flesh in the person of Jesus, came later in his life in the Italian village of Greccio located in the Rieti Valley between Rome and Assisi. Both St. Bonaventure and Thomas of Celano recount what happened there on Christmas Eve of 1223. Taking an excerpt from Celano, Francis spoke with a man named John from that region and said to him,

> If you desire to celebrate the coming feast of the Lord together at Greccio,…Hurry before me and carefully make ready the things I tell you. For I wish to enact the memory of that babe who was born in Bethlehem; to see as much as is possible with my own bodily eyes the discomfort of his infant needs, how he lay in a manger, and how, with an ox and an ass standing by, he rested on hay.[1]

This living nativity scene is what inspired the custom of the nativity sets that most Christians display in their homes at Christmastime. Note, as well, the very human picture of the infant Jesus that he gives, speaking of his resting on hay and having the discomfort of his infant needs. What is truly interesting about this event in Greccio, however, and as Franciscan scholar Brother William Short, OFM, points out is that while there were animals and people representing Mary and Joseph, there was no baby Jesus. The manger in Greccio was empty because it was under the altar where the Eucharist was celebrated.[2]

Francis instinctively made the connection between the Incarnation and the Eucharist and wanted to point out that is where Christ came alive in the people of Greccio. This is equally true for us today. Celebrating Christmas and the mystery of the Incarnation is not only about recalling what happened in Bethlehem over two thousand years ago, but it is also about allowing Christ to live in us today, and it is about encountering Him not only in the Eucharist but also in the poor and the marginalized and lowly ones of this world just as Francis demonstrated His presence to the lowly people of Greccio.

While the Christmas at Greccio near the end of Francis's life is the most concrete expression of his sense of the Incarnation, it is not the last word on the Franciscan sense of the Incarnation. There is so much more.

St. Francis was not a trained theologian, but he certainly had an intuitive grasp of the mysteries of faith, a grasp that came not from logic and reason but from the heart. As was pointed out earlier, later Franciscan theologians like St. Bonaventure and Blessed John Duns Scotus help us to flesh out and express in the language of theology the life experience of God that Francis had. I will attempt here to summarize briefly some theological insights on which Franciscan scholars have written volumes.

Most of us who are Christian were steeped in a theology of the Incarnation shaped by St. Anselm of Canterbury (1033–1109). Anselm wrote a famous work entitled *Cur Deus Homo?* Why did God become a Man? In this treatise, he answers that question basically by saying that only one who is both fully God and fully human can make satisfaction to an infinite God for the sins of humanity.[3] This is commonly called the atonement theory. It explains not only the Incarnation but also the Passion and Death of the Lord. What this approach basically says is that we humans messed up and so God had to send Jesus to bail us out. In this way of thinking, the Incarnation is merely a platform for Jesus's Passion and Death. Even before St. Francis, however, there was another line of thinking on the question of why God became human. That line of thinking basically says that God became human because He loves us and planned to become one of us right from the beginning even if we had not sinned. This may sound like heresy to many, but I assure you that it is not and that many of the theologians of the early Church held to this way of thinking. This does not mean that Jesus was not punished or that He did not take on the weight of our sins. He certainly did. What it does give us is a different perspective on why God became one of us. St. Irenaeus of Lyon in his work *Against Heresies* in the second century wrote, "Following the only true and steadfast Teacher, the Word of God, Our Lord Jesus Christ, who did, through His transcendent love become what we are, that He might bring us to be even what He is Himself."[4] Going back to the New Testament, both the prologue of John's Gospel and the letter to the Colossians lead us in the same direction. Thus, in the prologue of John's Gospel, we read,

> In the beginning was the Word, and the Word was with God, and the Word was God. All things came to be through him, and without him nothing came to be. What came to be through him was life, and this life was the light of the human race. (Jn. 1:1–4)

In the letter to the Colossians, we find the beautiful canticle on the preeminence of Christ,

> He is the image of the invisible God, the firstborn of all creation. For in him were created all things in heaven and on earth, the visible and the invisible, whether thrones or dominions or principalities or powers; all things were created through him and for him. He is before all things, and in him all things hold together. (Col. 1:15–17)

What John's Gospel, Colossians, and Irenaeus each tell is that God had a plan for humanity from the beginning, a plan that was carried out in and through Christ out of love. John tells us all is created for Christ as well. Seeing things in this way, one can see that it is entirely conceivable that, from the beginning, the Creator planned to be made manifest in creation. This happened in the person of Jesus Christ. The fact that we, in the meantime, had sinned certainly means that His coming is redemptive as well. Furthermore, if we can claim that all things are created through Christ and for him, as the letter to the Colossians says, then we can see that the coming of the Christ in the flesh is the culmination of the work of creation and not merely an intervention to fix what was broken.

Let's take a look now at how Francis himself and later Franciscan thinking pick up on this strain of theology.

In what we Franciscans call the Earlier Rule of St. Francis, we find many beautiful expressions of Francis's personal devotion, expressions which show how he understood God. One example of this is found in Chapter 23 of that rule where he writes,

> All powerful, most holy, Almighty and supreme God, Holy and just Father, Lord King of heaven and earth we thank you for yourself for through your holy will and through Your only Son with the Holy Spirit You have created everything spiritual and corporal..."

Further on, he continues,

> We thank You for as through Your Son You created us, so through Your holy love with which You loved us You brought about His birth as true God and true man by the glorious, ever-virgin, most blessed, holy Mary and you willed to redeem us captives through His cross and blood and death." [5]

Here, Francis appears to be saying that God loved us first and then redeemed us. It is thoughts like these that Bonaventure and Scotus would later develop theologically.

For those who are interested in pursuing a deeper understanding of Bonaventure and Scotus, I highly recommend the writings of Sr. Ilia Delio, OSF. She delves into the original writings of these two great Franciscan scholars and presents their thoughts in a clear and concise manner. For purposes of this book, I would simply like to underscore some of the points that she makes.

St. Bonaventure, inspired not only by Francis but also by several other theologians of his time such as Richard of St. Victor, sees God as total love. From this point of view, we see that our God is not a distant God who loves us when we need some loving, but is a God who loves us in motion. Love is part of the very essence of God. For Bonaventure, the Trinity is pure love with the Father, Son, and Spirit constantly exchanging love, a love which then expresses itself in the finite world through creation whose pinnacle is the Incarnate Christ. This all begins with what Bonaventure calls the fountain fullness of the Father's love. Sister Ilia gives us a beautiful example to explain this concept when she writes,

> An image of the Father to help us appreciate the first person of the Trinity is that of waterfalls. Anyone who has ever seen the torrents of gushing waters bursting forth over Niagara Falls has never failed to gasp in awe and wonder at the magnificent power of these waters. Imagine that the source of these bursting torrents of water is infinite. Such an image, although a limited one, gives us an idea of what the Father's infinite goodness is like. [6]

This image of flowing fullness carries out from the Father, Son, and Spirit and into creation and call us to move away from a "God up there somewhere" to a realization that through Christ, in whom all things are created, we are enveloped in the divine mystery of love. God then is both an awesome mystery and an intimate loving reality that touches us up close.[7]

I would point out again that though Francis himself never expressed his faith in such eloquent terms, Bonaventure is drawing on Francis's faith experience and his love for creation to develop this line of thinking.

Bonaventure never makes a direct statement in contradiction to the thought of the previously mentioned Anselm of Canterbury. In fact, in his early writings, he appears to embrace that line of thought though we can clearly see that later on, he saw the Incarnation as principally brought about as an expression of the Father's fountain fullness of love.

Duns Scotus, a Franciscan philosopher/theologian of the fourteenth century, does clearly state that even if there had been no sin, the Word would still have taken flesh. In a 2003 article in *Theological Studies*, Sister Ilia describes Scotus's thought in this way,

> For Scotus, therefore, the Incarnation takes place in light of God's glory and not in light of any sin which might be committed prior to the Incarnation. The Incarnation represents not a divine response to a human need for salvation but instead the divine intention from all eternity to raise human nature to

the highest point of glory by uniting it with divine nature. Scotus does not neglect sin and the need for redemption; however, he simply does not view sin as the reason for the Incarnation. Rather, the mutuality between God and human persons realized in the Incarnation is grounded in the very nature of God as love.[8]

The name commonly given to this line of thinking is the doctrine of the primacy of Christ. The word *primacy* does not simply mean that Christ is number on, as it were. All Christian theology states that. It rather refers to the fact that in Christ, all things are created and that all things flow from him (see Col. 1:15–20).

There are several implications from this theological perspective for those of us striving to follow a Franciscan spirituality.

First of all, it gives direction to our prayer life because we can both appreciate the majesty of God, God's transcendence if you will, and realize that God is at the same time infinitely close to us, loving us and always communicating with us in spite of our sin and weakness. This doesn't mean that we don't strive to turn away from sin, but rather that having been touched by such tremendous love, we less and less desire to sin.

A second implication for our spiritual journey is that we see the material world as good because it reflects the goodness of God and because it is all created in Christ right from the beginning.

A third implication is that we don't see ourselves as bearing Christ in a godless and sinful world but rather as pointing out the presence of Christ in all of God's creation even when that presence is not so obvious because of sin. I will draw out this notion more fully in a later chapter.

The Cross, Suffering, and Transformation

IN THE LAST chapter, we saw that Francis was deeply moved (wowed) by the mystery of the Incarnation and the humility of God, which it showed forth. That wonder at the mystery of the Incarnation reaches its culmination in the mystery of the Cross. The Cross plays a central role in Franciscan spiritual journey and in Franciscan spirituality. Early in his journey of conversion, he is praying before the crucifix in the church of San Damiano outside of Assisi where he receives the directive to go and repair the Lord's house.[1] In a later chapter on the Church, I will comment further on this mandate from the Lord. For now, however, the important point is that Christ crucified guided him from the very beginning though his contemplation and experience of the *Crucified*

One? would grow and deepen over the years. Near the end of his life after going through many trials both due to physical illness, struggles with Church leaders, and struggles and rejection even by his own brothers, he makes a retreat during September of 1224 with his close companion Brother Leo on Monte La Verna where he received the gift of the *stigmata*, the wounds of Christ imprinted on his own flesh.[2]

I do not wish in this book to delve into the issue of what exactly happened on Monte La Verna (Mt. Alvernia). I wish, more importantly, to reflect on the meaning of that experience for Francis and for us.

Francis's experience of the *Crucified One* is in keeping with the Franciscan experience of the Incarnation, which we saw in the previous chapter. Though at many times during his life, Francis is deeply aware of his sinfulness and openly lays claim to that, he does not go to the cross out of guilt for his sin but rather because of what Bonaventure calls, "The unconquerable enkindling of love in him for the good Jesus." Bonaventure further tells us that "He was being transformed into Him Who chose to be crucified out of the excess of His love.[3] Francis was no spiritual masochist seeking to suffer for suffering's sake. He encountered total unconditional love in the Crucified One and was transformed into an image of that love. For those of us striving to follow the Franciscan way, this is exactly how we are to approach the cross, contemplating the love that Jesus has for us and allowing ourselves to be transformed by that love. We may not literally bear the wounds of Christ in our bodies, but each in our own way, we will become living images of the loving Christ.

Interestingly, in John's Gospel at the beginning of Chapter 13, introducing the section that is commonly called the book of Glory, John writes, "He loved his own in the world, and He loved them to the end" (John 13:1). Jesus's mission then was to come in love and proclaim the reign of God. Because of sin, His offer of love is rejected. He did not come primarily to be punished. His mission was to come with unconditional love for us. That is how we are saved. Indeed, because we had sinned, that love was met with rejection. He neither runs away from the inevitable encounter with death and the cross nor does he lash out in anger against those who sentenced Him to death. Rather, He freely hands himself over. That, I believe, is the love which Francis encountered and wished to emulate.

In her book *Crucified Love*, which presents Bonaventure's approach to the Cross, Sr. Ilia Delio explains all of this very well. For those interested in exploring this thought more deeply, I highly recommend a careful reading of this book. She writes, for example, "For Bonaventure Christ Crucified *is* the mystery of God's love in the world that leads us into the very heart of the mystery of God."[4] She further writes,

> The idea that love is the principal reason of the passion rather than redemption makes the doctrine of the absolute primacy of Christ seem original to Bonaventure. While it is in some way implicit in his doctrine of the incarnation, Bonaventure does not

deny the historical circumstances of sin and, thus, maintains that satisfaction is an important reason for the incarnation, although it is not the primary reason. Rather, the primary reason for the incarnation is to manifest the power, wisdom, and glory of God. Nowhere are these manifested more powerfully than in the passion, death, and resurrection of Jesus Christ.[5]

The final point to be made with the Franciscan approach to the cross is to realize that as we are transformed, in love, into images of the Crucified One, we ourselves then strive to pour out ourselves in love to others.

The Eucharist

IN THE TWO previous chapters, we saw how Francis was deeply moved, perhaps we might say awestruck, by the humility of God in the mystery of the Incarnation and in the unconditional love that led Jesus to the cross. That same sense of awe and wonder carries over in Francis's sense of the Eucharist where the same Lord and Savior humbly comes to us in the form of bread and wine. In fact, Francis's understanding of the Eucharist is grounded in his sense of the Incarnation. Once the Word becomes flesh in the womb of Mary, the Word continues to be enfleshed in different ways. He saw the Word enfleshed in her because she bore Him in her womb.[1] Obviously, the Word is made flesh in the person of Jesus and, for Francis, that great mystery continues in the Church and in the Church above all in the Eucharist. This was quite clear at the wonderful Christmas event in Greccio, which took place at the Midnight Mass.

At the time of Francis, there were many who doubted the real presence of Christ in the Eucharist, a problem which continues to this very day. There were also many people who did not receive the Eucharist because of their lifestyle. Francis tried to address both of these issues. He likewise was very concerned about priests who were careless about their manner of celebrating the Eucharist, their caring for the sacred vessels, and their reserving the Eucharist in a dignified manner. What is important to remember is that his concern was generated by a deep faith in the gift of the Eucharist. He called people to do penance and confess their sins so that they could open themselves to receive what Francis called the Most Holy Body and Blood of the Lord. Likewise, I believe that he instinctively realized that part of the difficulty in believing that the Lord is truly present in the Eucharist is the fact that all too often His presence cannot be clearly seen in those who claim to believe in Him, a problem that is still with us today and that will be with us until the end of time.

There are several beautiful references to the Eucharist in the writings of Francis. One of the most powerful ones can be found in his Letter to the Entire Order where he writes,

> Let everyone be struck with fear, let the whole world tremble, and let the heavens exult when Christ, the Son of the living God, is present on the altar in the hands of a priest! O wonderful loftiness and stupendous dignity! O sublime humility! O humble

sublimity! The Lord of the universe, God and the Son of God so humbles Himself that for our salvation He hides Himself under an ordinary piece of bread! Brothers, look at the humility of God, and pour out your hearts before Him! Humble yourselves that you may be exalted by Him! Hold back nothing of yourselves for yourselves, that He who gives Himself totally to you may receive you totally.[2]

In reading and meditating on this passage, it becomes clear that Francis captured at a deep level an aspect of the Eucharist that can easily be lost, namely that this wonderful gift is meant to transform those of us who receive it, a transformation that takes place when those of us who receive the Eucharist give of ourselves to the Lord who then gives Himself to us. You may recall that, earlier in this book, I mentioned that surrender to God must be a part of any genuine spirituality. We know that Francis's life was one continual act of surrender and, here, it is clear that receiving the Eucharist for him was an act of surrender to Christ. Sometimes, although we deeply believe in the real presence of Christ in the Eucharist, we keep ourselves at a distance from Him. We may spend time in adoration and prayer before the Eucharist but do we open ourselves to Christ in this way every time that we go to Mass? Of course, over time, I believe that we are transformed even though we don't think in those terms because, after all, the good Lord can act on our lives even without our conscious participation in that action, but how much better it is when we seek that transformation. It is certainly a miracle that bread and wine are transformed into the Body and Blood of Christ, but how much more astounding that we too are transformed? The challenge is this—do we really want to be open to that transformation? I often listen to Catholic educational CDs from a company called Now You Know Media. To explore this dimension of the Eucharist more completely, I highly recommend a series that they produced by Fr. Dan Crosby, OFM, Cap. entitled *Becoming the Eucharist We Celebrate*.[3] In these recorded lectures, Father Dan shows how this aspect of the Eucharist was very clear in the earliest days of the Church. It became lost later on when we started emphasizing belief in the real presence of Christ in the Eucharist without sufficiently teaching the effects that this presence brings about.

Another dimension of the Eucharist, one which became highlighted with the Second Vatican Council, is the communal dimension of this wonderful sacrament. It is easy to fall into a so-called "me and Jesus" approach to the Eucharist, and it might seem, upon an initial reading, that Francis was prone to that kind of understanding. This, I think, is greatly due to the fact that theologians of the time did not emphasize the communal dimension of the Eucharist. In fact, it was not until the Second Vatican Council and the writings of some theologians prior to the council that this dimension, which has its roots in St. Paul, was reclaimed (see

1 Cor. 10:16–17). What we can say is that Francis's sense of the brotherhood and sisterhood of all creatures praising their Creator, which we will reflect on in a later chapter, had to have been nourished at least implicitly in his experience of Jesus becoming present in the bread and wine, gifts received from the hand of the Creator.

The Church

ONE OF THE great misconceptions of some readers of the life of Francis is to portray him as a rebel within the Church. To that I say, "Reformer, yes. Rebel, no." There is a difference. At the time of Francis, there were many groups that saw corruption within the Church and who desired to go back to a simpler form of Christianity, one that reflected more clearly the Gospels and the life of the early Church. These groups denounced the abuses in the Church and then left the Church. The genius of Francis is that he too saw the problems within the Church, but instead of leaving, he remained in the Church, and instead of rebelling, he, along with the early friars, Franciscan laity, and Poor Clares, modeled for the Church and the world how the Christian life was to be lived. The strength of this living witness certainly brought about, in rather rapid fashion, a real reform of the Church. The Church certainly did not become perfect, but it was indeed reformed.

In his rule, Francis insisted that the friars remain Catholic.[1] He instinctively realized that the Church was more than a mere human institution; that it is a divine mystery lived out by very weak human men and women. St. Paul calls the Church the Body of Christ in both Romans and First Corinthians (see both Rom. 12 and 1 Cor. 12), yet Paul realizes that the Body still needs to grow to its full stature (see Eph. 4:11–13).

Francis, because of what the Church and its theologians were emphasizing in the times in which he lived, does not tap in to Paul's imagery of the Church as the Body of Christ. His way of saying that the Church is the continuation of Christ's presence in the world after His death, resurrection, and ascension is his sense that the Word of God, the living Word, dwelt in the Church. As we saw in the previous reflection on the Incarnation, he had a deep reverence for the Word made flesh, which he beheld in the earthly body of Jesus as well as in the Eucharist. In his Salutation of the Blessed Virgin Mary, he refers to Mary as the "Virgin made Church."[2] What he expresses here is a realization that Mary was Church because the Word made flesh dwelt in her womb. For Francis, Church is where the Word dwells, be that the Scriptural Word, the Word made flesh in the Eucharist or the Word dwelling in the hearts of those who believe. In his Earlier Rule for the friars, he reflects on the parable of the sower and the seed, inviting the friars to empty themselves so that their hearts might be filled with the Word.[3]

For Francis, the Church, in spite of its sinful members, is also the dwelling place of the Word. It is also a more complete dwelling place to the extent that the Word is alive in more and more of its members. That is why, as we shall see in a later chapter, Francis insisted that his followers should be living witnesses of what they preach.

The reform of the Church then is accomplished by witness, by setting the example through the living of the Gospel rather than through protests. It also consists in helping the poor and the marginalized to realize that the Lord can and does dwell in them as well. I believe that Pope Francis, our present Jesuit pope who took the name of Francis, is calling the Church to the same kind of reform.

Finally, it should be clear from this that there is no Franciscan spirituality lived alone. It cannot be lived apart from the Church though it is lived in unique harmony between the Church and the marginalized people within and outside of the Church.

Part 2:
The Virtues of
Franciscan Spirituality

IN THE FIRST part of this work, I laid out what I believe to be the theological vision that shapes Franciscan life, be it the life of a friar, a sister, or a lay Franciscan. Vision alone, of course, can be just "pie in the sky." That vision must be expressed concretely in the way that we live. There are certain characteristics that mark one as Catholic, as Christian, and as Franciscans. The word that I like to use for such characteristics is *virtue*.

In our contemporary world, we often hear the word *values*. There is nothing wrong with having values, but virtue is something different. Virtue is the effort made to actually live a value. Living a virtuous life does not mean that one lives every virtue perfectly. It does mean that one is on the journey and is striving to live each virtue more and more completely.

There are certain virtues that ought to be part of any Christian life. Faith, hope, and charity are often called the theological virtues. There are likewise virtues like honesty, patience, prudence, etc., which ought to be part of any Christian life. In this section, I will not touch on these but rather on some virtues that I believe are uniquely Franciscan. I would add as well that there is an overlap in this list of virtues. Although I will reflect on them separately, you really cannot, as we shall see, separate poverty from minority, humility, penance, and the other virtues that will be touched upon because in the end, each of these is a reflection of Francis's desire to imitate the humility of God in Christ, the humility shown by giving Himself to us humans in the Incarnation, on the Cross, in the Church, and in the Eucharist.

The Spirit of Prayer and Devotion

As is the case with so much of Francis's writing, he never lays out for us a clear approach to prayer in the way that other great spiritual masters may have done. We can look at his writings, however, and find that there are some key elements to his approach to the life of prayer. One phrase that I think is unique to Francis is "the Spirit of holy prayer and devotion." He uses this expression in Chapter 5 of his rule for the friars as well as in his letter to St. Anthony, giving him permission to teach theology to the friars.[1] In both cases, he is using this expression in the context of work that the friars do. He is insistent that the friars should work for a living be it manual work or, as in the case of Anthony, teaching theology. Work, however, should not remove one from the Spirit of prayer and devotion but rather be integrated into that Spirit and be expressive of that Spirit.

Another key to understanding this expression is to note that the word *spirit* begins with a capital or uppercase letter *S*. That tells us that it is not just any spirit but the Holy Spirit present in and working through the labor of the friars and of anyone who is seeking to follow the Franciscan path. I would add here that while much reflection has been done over the years on other aspects of Franciscan life, this aspect of the work of the Spirit in our life and work could be developed even more, not only in Franciscan circles but also in the Church at large.

In his Earlier Rule in the chapter on prayer, Francis is writing in a very effusive and reflective way, and he says in the chapter dedicated to prayer:

> Therefore, let us desire nothing else, let us want nothing else, let nothing else please us and cause us delight except our Creator, Redeemer, and Savior, the only true God...Therefore, Let nothing hinder us, nothing separate us, nothing come between us. Wherever we are, in every place, at every hour, at every time of the day, every day and continually, let all of us truly and humbly believe, hold in our heart and love, honor, adore, serve, praise and bless, glorify and exult, magnify and give thanks to the Most High and Supreme Eternal God...[2]

The beauty of this is in its simplicity. Everyone can strive through everything that we do to be in touch with God and to praise and glorify God be it in more ecclesiastical ministry or manual work, white-collar work or work around the home.

Francis not only speaks of prayer but of prayer and devotion. The word *devotion*, I think, deserves some commentary. Catholics today are accustomed to various devotions in the form of the Rosary and various chaplets and novenas. Franciscans have been the originators of many of these devotions, but this is not what Francis is speaking of here. He is rather speaking of a wholehearted devotion and dedication to God in all that we do whether it be in formal prayer or in our work, much in the same way that we might say that a man or woman is totally devoted to their spouse, or that a soldier is devoted to his or her country.

Reading the above passages, one notes words like *praise*, *glorify*, *magnify*, among others. For our purposes here, I will stick to the word *praise* as summing up the other words and as another vital component of prayer for those who would follow Francis. As one looks through the prayers that Francis composed, we find that he is constantly praising God. We find this above all in His Praises of God as well as in the "Canticle of the Creatures," both of which I have included in an appendix at the end of this book.

Francis, in the above passage from the Earlier Rule also uses the word *desire*. He does not use that word frequently, but as is the case with all great spiritual teachers, the desire for God is a quintessential aspect of the life of prayer and of life in general. Recall that, at the beginning of this book, I cited Ronald Rolheiser's belief that spirituality is what we do with our desire. If that is the case, then desire, especially our desire and longing for union with God, must be expressed in our prayer. In fact, it is indeed the highest form of prayer.

The final aspect of prayer that we note in Francis is humility. As was pointed out earlier in this work for him, God is Most High, and we are little ones as we stand before God.

For us Franciscans, then there is no clear "methodology" for prayer, but in all that we do, the Spirit is at work in us, enabling us to praise and glorify God as humble little ones at every moment of every day.

Penance

WE FRANCISCANS ARE to be counted among those who do penance. Francis had a unique understanding of that word. In popular religious language, we have, unfortunately, come to think of penance as some type of punishment or sacrifice in which we engage in order to atone for our sins. Although that is certainly a dimension of penance, it does not reflect the deepest meaning of that word. The root meaning of penance can be found in the Gospels, especially in the beginning of Mark's Gospel where we are told, "After John had been arrested, Jesus came to Galilee proclaiming the Gospel of God: This is the time of fulfillment. The Kingdom of God is at hand. Repent, and believe in the Gospel" (Mk. 1:14–15). Repent, in this invitation, translates the Greek *metanoia*/ μετάνοια. It means "to turn around one's life, to turn away from the values of the world, and to live by the values of the Gospel." I believe that St. Francis understood penance in this way when he called his first followers the brothers and sisters of penance, a term still claimed today by the secular (lay) Franciscans.

The English word *repent* in the Gospels also translates the Greek word *metamellomai* /μεταμέλλομαι. This Greek word basically means "a sorrowful regret for one's actions." Unfortunately, Christian practice over the centuries has emphasized this latter meaning of repentance at the expense of the former. Francis himself at times repented in this way when he would fast and make other sacrifices to repent for his sins. In his writings, he often exhorts the friars and others to repent in this way. Near the end of his life, however, he asked forgiveness of "Brother Ass," as he called his body,[1] realizing that he had gone too far in treating his body harshly.

I make these points because in living a Franciscan spirituality today, I believe that while the asceticism of the second approach to penance has its place, the real call to penance is that of radically turning away from the values of this world and embracing the values of the Gospel and the close following of Jesus that it calls for. For me, ascetical practices and self-mortification cannot be an end in themselves. They are useful only insofar as they help us in living a Gospel life instead of the life the world would have us live.

I find this to be a particularly strong challenge today because it calls us out of the idolatry of political and ideological loyalty. The Franciscan, and anyone else for that matter, who seeks to live the Gospel cannot be considered either fully liberal or fully conservative by political standards. For that matter, it would probably be foolhardy to totally embrace any political philosophy over the Gospel. While there are values on both sides of the political spectrum that reflect the Gospel, neither of these positions does so completely. As followers of Jesus in the footsteps of Francis, we stand outside of the sphere of political ideologies and agendas. This will win us the adulation of some, the opposition of many, and the confusion of many more.

The three vows of poverty, chastity, and obedience, taken not only by Franciscans but also by all Catholic religious as well as some in other Christian denominations are, when lived properly, radical statements that money and possessions, the pursuit of pleasure, and the gaining of power are not and cannot be the primary focus of our lives. When they are, they become idols. Choosing not to worship these and other idols and living accordingly even without formally taking vows is at the heart of what it means to live a life of penance.

For all of us, doing the penance of living the Gospel is a lifelong task. None of us are doing it perfectly. Growing with this task is a lifelong journey.

Poverty

Perhaps the one word most commonly associated with the name Franciscan is *poverty*. Francis himself was known as *Il Poverello*, "the poor one." Living as a poor one, especially in the United States and in other parts of the western world today, presents us with real challenges, yet they are challenges that must be met if we are to truly call ourselves Franciscan.

One of the risks in trying to explain poverty as an evangelical and Franciscan virtue is that one could seem to not only explain it but to also explain it away. I hope to avoid that here.

Let's begin by saying what Franciscan poverty is not. It is not living in misery and squalor. Too many people in today's world live in subhuman conditions. If anything, Franciscan poverty must include helping people who live in these conditions to move out of them and to live simple but dignified fully human lives. I am happy to say that while working in Bolivia and in places like the Bronx and Camden, NJ, I saw my fellow friars doing exactly that.

To understand what Francis meant by poverty, I believe that we need only to turn to the opening lines of the Rule of 1223, the rule of life that we friars have professed to live for nearly eight hundred years. Francis says there, "The Rule and Life of the Lesser Brothers is this: to observe the Holy Gospel of Our Lord Jesus Christ by living in obedience, *without anything of one's own*, and in chastity."[1]

That highlighted phrase "without anything of one's own," which translates the Latin *sine proprio* is, I believe, the key to understanding and living poverty as a Franciscan be it as a vowed religious or as a lay person. To share some of my own experience like most religious of my age, I came into the order at a time when the living of all of our vows was spelled out in a legalistic way. One was allowed to have a certain amount of money, to have certain items in your room for your use and one had to ask permission for anything extra. As long as one was living within the parameters of laws and permissions, one was living the vows including poverty. This led to a very external and superficial understanding not only of poverty but also of all of the vows that we profess.

As the Second Vatican Council came upon us with its call for religious to go back to the spirit of their founder, we rediscovered some of the richness and wisdom that Francis had passed on to us. We asked, "What does it mean to live without anything of one's own?" We discovered that it was a radical choice not to claim ownership of anything even opinions and ideas but most importantly to realize that all that is given for our use is a gift.

Now a shallow understanding of this notion that all is a gift would be to have a vast array of money and possessions and to simply say, "Well, it is all a gift." Nothing could be further from the truth. An encounter that I had with an elderly woman in Maine many years ago illustrates well what is meant by this idea. I was preaching a parish mission and, as is the custom of our Ministry of the Word preaching team to visit the homebound of the parishes where we preach, I visited her in her home. The house was a simple bungalow and there was a car, at least ten years old, parked in the driveway. Inside, the home was neat, sparsely furnished, and spotlessly clean. When I asked her how she was doing, her answer astounded me with its wisdom. She said, "Father, The Lord has blessed me with an abundant sufficiency." She captured in those words what I believe is meant by evangelical poverty. She saw her simple possessions as more than enough. She was grateful for them, and she didn't need any more. For me, those were words to live by. Whether one has a formal vow of poverty, as I do, or one is simply trying to live a simple life as a lay person, that is a great attitude to have. When one is grateful for the little things that he or she has, one does not seek more, and if more comes along, it is a gift to be used in keeping with living a Gospel way of life. Her example has guided me in recent years to be grateful not only for the items given for my use—books, computers, even an automobile—but also to appreciate the gift of the beauty around me. I can walk along Tampa Bay every day that I am home in St. Petersburg. There is much beauty to behold there—the water, the dolphins that leap up occasionally, the exotic tropical birds. It is all a gift from God. I don't need to own it.

Not long ago, I finished reading a wonderful book by the German theologian Johannes B. Metz entitled *Poverty of Spirit*. It would be beyond the scope of this book to analyze his work in depth, but some of the main points of his book are well worth mentioning.[2]

Metz speaks of the poverty of Jesus in the terms mentioned in Paul's letter to the Philippians:

> Though he was in the form of God, [he] did not regard equality with God something to be grasped, Rather, he emptied himself, taking the form of a slave, coming in human likeness; and found himself human in appearance, he humbled himself, becoming obedient to death, even death on a cross. (Phil. 2:6–8)

For Metz, the poverty of Jesus is reflected in this passage, the poverty of becoming human. He goes on to make the point that evangelical poverty of spirit comes in imitating the poverty of Christ by embracing our humanity in all of its limitations. He goes in depth about what this means, and I would suggest reading his work for anyone who wishes to live the virtue of evangelical poverty.

Returning to St. Francis, you may recall that in an earlier chapter, we reflected on his sense of God's greatness and his own smallness in relationship to that. This perspective goes hand in hand with what Metz has to say and is, I believe, the core of what Franciscan poverty is about, namely imitating the poverty of Christ in all that we do. Grounded in this perspective, one need not worry so much about what one has and does not have because, like Jesus, we live "without anything of our own" and can claim with my friend from Maine that we indeed do have "an abundant sufficiency."

Minority—Being Little
Among God's Little Ones

THOSE OF US who belong to the first order of St. Francis are known as Friars Minor, thus the initials after our names—OFM—for Order of Friars Minor. After explaining where the name Minor comes from, I would like, in this chapter, to speak of "minority" as a virtue that all Franciscans are called to live.

In Francis's day in the early thirteenth century, there were two classes of people in a town like Assisi, the *maiores* (or "powerful ones—the *majors*," if you will) and the *minores* ("*the minors*, the little ones, those excluded from power"). It is important to understand that while Francis came from a family of wealthy merchants, they did not belong to the class of *maiores* because though they had wealth, they did not have much power. People like Francis's father sought to move themselves into that ruling class. He believed that if people like his son could win glory as knights going to battle, then this would help to move them up the social ladder. When Francis failed to win such honors, his father was disappointed and even embarrassed. In a well-known scene, which was a turning point in Francis's life, after his father had complained that he was giving away goods to the poor and not behaving like a member of the upper classes, he was brought before the bishop. Francis then stripped himself naked, gave his clothes back to his father, and declared that from that point on, he had "no father except Our Father in heaven."[1]

With this powerful gesture, Francis definitively began his journey of living *sine proprio* though, indeed, that journey had begun even earlier. With this gesture, he also affirmed his littleness as a creature before God, something reflected upon earlier in this book, and surrendered as well any thought of counting himself among the *maiores*. Because of this, he came to identify with the *minors* and sought together with his brothers to show the little ones that God loved and cared for them, that God dwelt not only in monasteries and fancy churches but also among them as well.

For Franciscans, the term *minority* in so many ways sums up what Franciscan life is all about because it not only calls us to live simply ourselves as minors but also to identify with the struggles that all those who are excluded from places of power and inclusion in our society. Pope Francis has never used the term minority in this sense. But is constantly calling the whole Church to a life of minority. He invites us to do things like heading for the exit signs of the Church, going out into the streets, and seeking out those who are not only materially poor but also those who feel marginalized and excluded from the Church and from society for many different reasons.

In Francis's time, it was the lepers above all who represented those who were marginalized. They were considered unclean and lived well outside the walls of the city. The mere sight of them was repulsive to Francis as a young man. At one point, however, he came across a leper, came down from his horse, and embraced him. He then actually spent some time living with the lepers.[2] This experience was so profound that it marks for Francis a major turning point in his life. In the Testament of St. Francis, he tells us,

> When I was in sin it seemed too bitter for me to see lepers. And the Lord Himself led me among them and I showed mercy to them. And when I left them, what had seemed bitter to me was tuned into sweetness of soul and body.[3]

Today, it is the homeless, the immigrant, and the victims of aids, Ebola, and other terrible diseases, as well as those who feel that they have no place in the Church that might figuratively be considered as being lepers. Being minors calls us to walk with those people and to assure them that God loves them and dwells among them and calls them to follow His Son as well. This is done in imitation of Christ who became poor to walk with us on our journey of life.

Spiritual Nakedness

I WOULD LIKE to begin this chapter by assuring the reader that I am not suggesting that anyone remove their clothing in public although Francis himself did that on a few occasions. In the previous chapter, I mentioned his stripping of himself before the bishop of Assisi, the mayor, and his father. This was not an act of rebellion so much as a radical statement that he claimed nothing of his own, even the clothing on his back, that he would live, from that moment on, *sine proprio*, as we saw previously. In the same spirit, as he was dying in the company of his brothers, he had all of his clothing removed so that he could go back to God in the same condition in which he entered the world.[1]

By claiming nakedness as a Franciscan virtue, I am referring to the sense of Franciscans being "real" and being "down to earth" as I mentioned in the beginning of this book. This is one of the things that drew me to want to join the friars, and it still draws people to the Franciscans. Perhaps another way of stating this is to say, in the words of Pope Francis, that Franciscans, above all, are to have "the smell of the sheep" on them. What I think the pope is saying when he uses this expression is that, as Christians, we are not to stand above the fray, looking down on the weak and the sinful, but rather as fellow sinners ourselves, we are to walk with them, identifying with their struggles. In many ways, this is the same thing as being a minor that we spoke about in the last chapter, yet it adds another dimension to it. Nakedness suggests that we go about stripped of any pretense of superiority due to our office, our educational degree, or anything else that might put us in a position of superiority over others.

To be naked in this sense also means a complete refusal to engage in clericalism. While this certainly presents a challenge to someone like me who is a priest and who has a graduate education, I have noticed that it is a challenge even for those who are neither ordained nor members of religious orders, but who have leadership responsibilities in the Church, and who act as though they were above the people they serve. Once again referring to Pope Francis, we would do well to heed his warnings against lay clericalism as well. Perhaps rather than using the word *clericalism*, we can say that the Franciscan person goes about stripped of all pretensions.

Referring back to our reflection on poverty as part of the Franciscan life, I believe that it is this quality of *nakedness* that truly marks us as being among God's poor ones.

Love of Creation

OVER THE YEARS, much has been made of St. Francis as a lover of animals, birds, and nature in general. In fact, that is how most people think of Francis. That is why so many churches, not just Franciscan ones, conduct a blessing of animals on or around the feast of St. Francis on October 4. Some folks refer to this aspect of his life as "Francis of the bird bath." While a quick reading of his life would tell you that there is some truth to this understanding, I would like to suggest here that the Franciscan love for creation is something much deeper than that.

To understand the deeper connection between Francis and creation, I think that we need to look to a time near the end of his life when he composed the well-known "Canticle of the Creatures." As I pointed out earlier in this book, the first impression that one might get upon reading this beautiful poem is that is the work of a young dreamer. While Francis was indeed a dreamer in his youth, the poem was actually written toward the end of his life.

As I noted previously, Francis was spending time in a small cell outside the convent of the Poor Clares. He was suffering from various illnesses but most especially an illness to his eyes that made it nearly impossible for him to behold the light of the sun. It was at this time that he was assured in prayer of his salvation and of his place in the kingdom. As a result of this assurance, he desired to compose a hymn of praise to the Lord for his creatures. Thus we are told that he told his companions who were with him at this difficult time,

> Therefore for His praise, for our consolation and for the edification of our neighbor, I want to write a new *Praise of the Lord* for his creatures, which we use every day, and without which we cannot live. Through them the human race greatly offends the Creator, and every day we are ungrateful for such great graces, because we do not praise, as we should, Our Creator and the Giver of all good.[1]

For me, the words which Francis utters here are prophetic and indicative of what many modern theologians are saying regarding a truly Christian approach to creation and the environment. For too long, many people have used Genesis 1:26 ("Let them have dominion over the fish of the sea, the birds of the air, and the cattle, and all the wild animals and all the creatures that crawl on the ground") as an excuse for plundering the fish, the animals, and the environment for selfish reasons. It is obvious that Francis was well aware of that fact eight centuries ago when he accuses humans of offending the Creator by such abuse. Reliance solely on this verse from Genesis as the basis for human relationship to creation has led to a concept of separation between humans and the rest of creation. In such an understanding, we become the subjects who act upon nature and who unfortunately do so with impunity for our own selfish ends. It also feeds into the notion that the rest of creation was put here, and we were then placed over and above that creation. It suggests as well that the rest of creation has no intrinsic value and has worth only insofar as it serves human need. A proper understanding of this passage would suggest that the dominion over creatures given to us is to be an imitation of God's dominion and not one motivated by selfish ends.

Many theologians across the spectrum of Christianity today point out that the above-cited line from Genesis is not the only place in the Bible that offers a perspective on the relationship of humans and the rest of creation. Moreover, due to modern science, we now understand clearly that we are made from the same stuff that burst forth when the universe came into being over thirteen billion years ago. Elizabeth Johnson in her book *Ask the Beasts*[2] delves into this fact, and I would encourage anyone who wishes to explore this thought further to read her book. She—as well as many other theologians not only recently but also throughout the history of Christianity—likewise point out that the Scriptures also state that the other creatures have an inherent dignity not only because they are created by God but also because God as Creator is present in and through the other creatures. One such example can be found in the Book of Wisdom.

> For you love all things that are and loathe nothing that you have made; for what you hated you would not have fashioned. And how could a thing remain unless you willed it; or be preserved, had it not been called forth by you? But you spare all things that are yours, O Lord and lover of souls, for your imperishable spirit is in all things. (Ws 11:24–12:1)

She also cites not only modern theologians but also voices like those of Augustine and Thomas Aquinas who show that God as Creator is at the same time above the universe and within every single creature.

It seems that Francis, not through any formal study of Scripture and theology, simply had what we might call a gut sense of the relationship between us humans and the rest of creation, which is why, in the Canticle of the Creatures, he can call created things his brothers and sisters. He was aware, as we have seen that as a fellow creature, he had a special bond with "Brother Sun and Sister Moon." In this canticle, we see as well that not only are the creatures his brothers and sisters but also those who can and do join him in praising God. This concept, by the way, is not new to Francis. Those of us who pray the Liturgy of the Hours (the Divine Office, the breviary) regularly pray the canticle of the three youths that is found in the book of Daniel (Dan. 3:57–88). In this canticle, all of God's creatures are called upon to give praise to the Lord.

It is important, finally, to note that while this strain of Franciscan spirituality has been around for eight centuries, it is being called into the forefront today for several reasons. One is that there is now an ongoing debate about what might be called either global warming or climate change. This debate has been highly politicized by both conservatives and liberals. A spiritual-theological approach not only to this debate but also to the overall understanding of the human relationship to creation is, I believe, vitally important. Why not then let the Franciscan vision be considered as the basis for that? I think that this is why, in 1979, Pope St. John Paul II declared St. Francis to be the patron saint of ecology.[3] In this regard, as this book was being prepared for publication, Pope Francis issued his now well publicized encyclical *Laudato Si.* The title is taken directly from the opening line of the Canticle of the Creatures. A great deal of the commentary on this work has been focused on the pope's embrace of climate change. This misses the point. The real issue is that the encyclical calls for a renewed awareness of our place in creation and our relationship to the Creator. In this wonderful work, all of humanity is called to embrace what is basically the Franciscan vision of the universe. Pope Francis's message can basically be summed up in a statement he made at his Innaugural Mass

Protect creation...protect all creation, the beauty of the created world...respect each of God's creatures and respect the environment in which we live...care for creation and for our brothers and sisters...protect the whole of creation, protect each person, especially the poorest...Let us protect with love all that God has given us.[4]

Something that is very interesting here is that Pope Francis links the concern for creation with concern for the poor. I see, in this connection, a Franciscan awareness of the bond between all of God's creatures. We cannot separate ourselves from the poor. We are one with them. This I find to be both an affirmation and a challenge for those of us striving to live a Franciscan spirituality.

Brotherhood/Sisterhood

IF WE CLOSELY study the life of Francis, we can see that, at the beginning of his period of turning to God, after his time as a soldier and his imprisonment, he had no intention of starting a religious order. He simply wished to follow Jesus more closely and serve Him in whatever way was necessary. In time, other people, many of whom were the companions of his youth, came to join him. Almost immediately, he called them his brothers. Even then, he did not form them into a formal religious community. It was only after they started going around and preaching that he was impelled, in the year 1209, to travel to Rome and ask permission of Pope Innocent III to live a Gospel life.[1] In the Testament of St. Francis, written near the end of his life, he tells us, "And after the Lord gave me brothers no one told me what to do but the Most High Himself revealed to me that I should live according to the pattern of the Gospel."[2]

I have refrained from too much speculation about Francis in the writing of this book and have tried to base my thoughts on the facts of his life. That having been said, I have often wondered about the effects on him of being rejected by his father and also of not having any siblings, at least none that have been reported to us. I think that he probably found in the men who joined him in those early days of the order the family that he never had. They truly became his brothers, and he related to them accordingly.

This sense of brotherhood also extended to those who would be leaders in the Franciscan communities. He eschews titles like *abbot* and *prior*, titles which suggest superiority, and prefers instead titles like *minister* and *guardian* because the leaders were older brothers and not superiors. This is expressed clearly in one of his Admonitions, words that he passed on to the friars over a period of years in the early days of the order. In one of these Admonitions, he writes, "Let those who are placed over others boast about that position as much as if they were assigned the duty of washing the feet of their brothers."[3]

From this early experience, brotherhood became a core value for him and became not only the way in which he related to the other friars but also his a way of relating to everyone and everything even, as we saw previously, to all the other creatures in God's creation.

You may have noted in the quote from his Admonitions that he refers to "washing the feet of the brothers." It is important to note for English speakers that the word *friar* literally means "brother," as it is derived from the Latin word *frater* and the French word *frère*.

Broadening out this notion of brotherhood to other religious and to lay people who wish to follow the Franciscan way, I believe that every Franciscan man or woman is called to relate to all other people and all creatures as their brother or sister and to be a sister or brother for all. I have found this not only to be a beautiful concept but also a real challenge both in the friaries where I have lived and among the people I have been called to serve in ministry. After all, even in the best of families, getting along with our siblings can be a difficult. Being a brother to all, for me, is a call to minority and humility and is vital to living a Franciscan life.

For those who do not live the formally vowed life, and also for those who are not members of the Secular Franciscan Order, I would urge you to find a few folks who can more closely be your brothers and sisters and to meet with them occasionally to share your life of faith and, above all, to pray with them.

Being a brother or sister then is not a matter of having a canonical title. It is how we relate to the world and to all of God's creation.

Always Preaching

"ALWAYS PREACH, SOMETIMES use words." This sentiment is often attributed to Francis, and while it does not appear as such in any of his writings, it sums up his approach to preaching namely that if one dares to preach one's life ought to be consistent with the message proclaimed. Throughout his life, Francis exhorts the friars to preach by example when they entered the town of Assisi as well as other towns where they went to preach. We know that Jesus Himself warned against hypocrisy many times so that the concept of preaching by example is certainly not new to Francis, but it certainly was emphasized by him. One place in his writings that clearly expresses this notion can be found in the Earlier Rule of the order written in 1221. In a chapter dedicated to preachers, after reminding the friars that they are to preach verbally only with permission of Church authorities and their own superiors, he writes, "Let all the brothers, however, preach by their deeds."[1] Later in that same chapter, he exhorts them to be humble when they preach, attributing all things to God and not to themselves.

What is perhaps overlooked in this exhortation to let all preach by their deeds is the fact that not all of the brothers (friars) were clerics who would have the permission to preach in liturgical settings. There are two important implications deriving from this fact. The first is that many of the early friars who were not clerics did preach, not during the liturgy but in town squares and other public places. This is evident from reading any of the early lives of Francis. This means that many of them did have permission to engage in this type of preaching. Thus, in his Later Rule, he exhorts those who preach "that their language be well considered and chaste for the benefit and edification of the people, announcing to them vices and virtues, punishment and glory, with brevity, because our Lord when on earth kept his word brief."[2] I don't believe with the exception of the exhortation to brevity that these words were intended for friar priests who preached liturgically. They obviously would have had to go beyond the parameters set down there. He is speaking here of the friars, clerics and nonclerics alike, who were, for lack of a better term, marketplace preachers.

I make this point about nonclerical preaching because this book is not just for clerics. In fact, I would hope that the vast majority of those reading it are not clerics. In our times, there are many lay people who engage in a new style of marketplace preaching. They do so at parish missions and days of recollection as well as at other public-speaking occasions. In addition to that, there are so many opportunities in day-to-day conversation to "proclaim the Word." The pulpit is not the only place where that is done. I think that Francis's exhortations to preachers apply in a broad sense to all of us, clerics and laity alike, who would preach by example and sometimes with words.

I would like to call attention to one other dimension not only of Franciscan preaching but also of any kind of ministry in which we engage. In the earlier chapters on Incarnation and Creation, it was made clear that we Franciscans view the whole world, indeed the whole universe, as manifesting the presence of Christ. This has tremendous implications for the way that we conduct ourselves with others, especially those who do not believe. There can be a temptation to a kind of spiritual arrogance for preachers and others engaged in ministry to go about with an attitude of "I have Jesus, and you don't." Now it may be true that someone else does not believe in Jesus or even outright rejects Him. Nonetheless, Jesus is present everywhere, including in that person. He is likewise present even in the most horrible and deplorable and evil situations that this life has to offer. Witness the many Jews and Christians who maintained their faith and found God and Jesus even in the concentration camps. While I certainly understand and would not judge those who lost their faith in those horrible places, the point I am trying to make is that from a Franciscan perspective Christ is always present everywhere and in everyone even if He is buried under a heap of sin and corruption. Our task, whether preaching or in any other ministry, is not so much to bring Christ to the situation but to call Him forth. This attitude is also an expression of the minority and brotherhood/sisterhood, which we reflected on previously.

Instruments of Peace

Most folks know of the peace prayer of St. Francis, which begins with the words, "Make me an instrument of Your Peace." This prayer was composed in honor of St. Francis sometime in the late 1800s and became the official prayer of the League of Nations when it was formed after World War I. Though this prayer was composed well after Francis's lifetime, it clearly captures his spirit in so many ways.

Francis himself did not know peace as a young man. He experienced rejection by his father that came to a head in the previously mentioned meeting with the bishop and his father when he stripped himself. His father was known to be a strong willed and violent man. In addition to that, although we do not have many details, he experienced the horrors of war firsthand. Coming from that experience, we find that very shortly after his conversion, he would go about preaching and, in his preaching, say, "May the Lord give you peace."[1] Implied in this statement are two important things. First of all is the fact that real peace comes from the Lord and through faith in Him. His preaching was very simple. It consisted of an invitation to a life of penance. As we have already seen, this meant not so much acts of self-denial but rather a turning away from the ways of the world, ways which too often included violence as a means of solving problems.

One interesting moment in Francis's ministry came when he was passing near the town of Arezzo, which was being shaken by a civil war. Francis, we are told by St. Bonaventure, saw demons dancing over the city. He sent a friar priest named Sylvester into the city to command the devils to leave. Sylvester did so, and the city returned to peace.[2] It was that civil strife that led Francis to discern that there were devils present. He instinctively knew that discord and violence open people up to all sorts of evil.

Francis would travel with the crusaders to places like Egypt and Syria not to fight battles but to preach the Gospel. He did so with the expectation that he would meet a martyr's death. That would not happen. What did happen is that he had the opportunity to preach to the sultan, Malek-al-Kamil, at Damietta in Egypt. Though he did not succeed in converting this man who could have had him killed, he did win his respect and admiration as being truly a man of God and of peace.[3] For those interested in a more in-depth look at this wonderful moment in Francis's life, I highly recommend a book recently published by Paul Moses entitled *The Saint and the Sultan: The Crusades, Islam and Francis of Assisi's Mission of Peace.* That work is referenced in the bibliography at the end of this book.

Francis's mission of peace continued right up until the time of his death. At that time, we are told in a work called *The Legend of Perugia* that there had been a clash between the bishop of Assisi and the 'podesta' (basically "the mayor"). Though very ill, he added another verse to the "Canticle of the Creatures," "Praised be You, my Lord, through those who give pardon for Your love, and bear infirmity and tribulation. Blessed are those who endure in peace for by You, Most High, shall they be crowned."[4] After composing this verse, he had the friars go through the town reciting these words. After this, there was indeed peace between the two, and Francis would die in a town at peace.

What then does Francis's commitment to peace say to us? To me, it is quite clear that building peace is an integral part of Franciscan spirituality. In a conversation that I recently had with my confrere Dan Lanahan, OFM, we talked not only about peacemaking, but as Dan said, "Peacebuilding." I believe that in the life and actions of St. Francis, we find both. It is obvious that he was a peacemaker at Arezzo and he was also responsible for bringing the mayor and the bishop together in Assisi. Peacebuilding on the other hand is what is done to create an atmosphere of peace so that conflict does not arise in the first place. This we saw in Francis's encounter with the sultan. He did not go in with guns blazing and call him an infidel and a sinner. He went and humbly spoke the message of the Gospel, and as we have seen previously, though the Sultan did not convert, he saw in Francis a true man of God. Interestingly, in the Earlier Rule, he writes,

> As for the brothers who go, they can live spiritually among the Saracens (Muslims) and nonbelievers in two ways. One way is not to engage in arguments or disputes but to be subject to every human creature for God's sake and to acknowledge that they are Christians. The other way is to announce the Word of God, when the see it pleases the Lord, in order that unbelievers might believe in almighty God, etc.[5]

What great wisdom is found here! Francis does not encourage missionaries to rush into places, denouncing the sins and errors of its inhabitants, but rather to use prudence and wisdom and guidance from the Lord to discern when to proclaim the Word, when to speak out. This is peacebuilding at its best. How many problems might have been avoided had this approach been used for example at the time of the Reformation or in the lead up to the many wars that we humans have had?

I rejoice at the example given to us by Pope Francis in this regard, in his dealing with all sorts of people with whom we Catholics may disagree. He still approaches them and respects their human dignity as a first step before noting the differences that we might have. This is indeed a challenge for

Christians but an even stronger one for the leaders of nations in today's world.

Finally, I call to mind the opening line of a popular hymn, "Let there be peace on earth and let it begin with me." While we can certainly hope that world leaders would commit to peacebuilding and peacemaking, it is essential that each of us as individuals commit to this path in dealing with the many conflicts and disputes that we have in our own lives.

Conclusion—The Perfect Joy of Living the Gospel

With all that has been said in this book, the bottom line is that living a Franciscan life is about living the Gospel. While it is obvious that in the end any Christian spirituality is about living the Gospel, Francis, as we saw previously, makes it abundantly clear right at the beginning of his rule, which states, "The Rule and Life of the Lesser Brothers is this: to observe the Holy Gospel of our Lord Jesus Christ by living in obedience, without anything of one's own, and in chastity."[1]

It is important to understand what is meant by "living the Gospel." It is not just a matter of literally living out the various teachings of Matthew, Mark, Luke, and John, although Francis does quite a bit of that. It is rather radically to base one's life on the belief that Jesus Christ is the Son of God and that He became human, lived, suffered, died, and rose from the dead that we might have life. This is the sense of the word *gospel* that is found in St. Paul before the four Gospels were even written. Thus Paul writes,

> Now I am reminding you, brothers, of the gospel I preached to you, which you indeed received, and in which also you stand. Through it you are also being saved, if you hold fast the word I preached to you, unless you believed in vain. For handed on to you as of first importance what I also received, that Christ died for our sins in accordance with the Scriptures, that He was buried; that He was raised on the third day in accordance with the Scriptures. (1 Cor. 15:1–4)

Gospel literally means "good news," and the good news is that we are given life and salvation through Jesus Christ. At the time of Francis, that basic message, while certainly not lost, was hidden behind a thousand other concerns as, unfortunately, it often is today. The four evangelists whose Gospels are part of the Scriptures flesh out for us how Jesus lived out this message and prepared his followers to receive and live it.

Everything spelled out in this book is a way of showing how Francis and all who would follow his way of life strive to live the Gospel. Being poor, being minors, having a spirit of prayer and devotion, etc., are not ends in themselves but means of living the Gospel, the "good news of salvation." The result in our lives of claiming this message and living this way should be *joy*. In John's Gospel, Jesus tells us, "I have told you this [*this* being His proclamation of His love for us and His call to love each other] so that my joy may be in you and your joy may be complete" (John 15:11).

Among the many great contributions of the Franciscan way to the world and to the Church has been, and still is, the witness of showing that living a Christian life produces joy. Too many Christians, as Pope Francis tells us are people "whose lives seem like Lent without Easter."[2]

His apostolic exhortation is called *Evangelii Gaudium*, which means "The Joy of the Gospel". It is a proclamation of joy as the principal fruit of living the Gospel. This is vitally important in a world where religion all too often seems joyless and where joy and happiness are proclaimed as coming from money, power, and the pursuit of pleasure. There is nothing wrong with these three things in themselves. It's just that they can never be the root source of meaning in our lives.

A question that may arise from this is, "What is Joy?" St. Francis had an answer to this question when he engaged Brother Leo, one of his early companions, in a discussion about this topic. The text of this conversation presented to us in a work called *The Fioretti* or *The Little Flowers of St. Francis* will be included in the appendix at the end of this book. The gist of the story is that Francis wore out poor Leo by telling him that the great holiness of the friars and their many successes would not constitute perfect joy. Leo, were he alive today, would probably have said, "Well then, what the heck is perfect joy?" Francis answer was that if they were to knock on a friary door late on a rainy night and be thrown out and cursed by the friar who answered the door, then that would be perfect joy.

For many of us friars, this story has been the source of humor causing us to role our eyes when a superior or another friar treats us poorly. We laugh and say, "Okay, that's perfect joy for you." Francis, however, is not teaching us to be masochists who seek out misery and poor treatment. The real moral of the story is that if we have truly internalized the truth of the Gospel and grounded our life in the "good news," then we have something that not even the worst mistreatment can take away. That, my friends, is truly a cause for joy.

Joy then is not happiness, giddiness, or just having fun. Those things are great, but they are passing. True joy comes from having something that gives ultimate meaning to our lives even in the face of great adversity.

I pray for all who read this short book that following Francis and living the Gospel will produce lasting joy in your life.

Notes

Spirituality and Religion

1. Roy Gasnick, OFM, *The Francis Book*, (New York: Collier Books, a Division of MacMillan Publishing Company, New York, 1980), p. 121.

2. St. Bonaventure of Bagnoreggio, "The Major Legend," Chapter 14, in *Francis of Assisi: The Founder*, volume 2 of *Francis of Assisi: Early Documents*, eds. Regis Armstrong, OFM, Cap., J. A. Wayne Hellman, OFM, Conv., and William J. Short, OFM (New York: New City Press, 2000), p. 642.

3. Pew Forum on Religion and Public Life, "Nones" on the Rise, October 9, 2012.

4. Ronald Rolheiser, *The Holy Longing* (New York: Doubleday, 1999), p. 7.

5. Ibid.

6. St. Augustine, *Confessions*, 1, I, tran. by Henry Chadwick (Oxford: Oxford University Press, 1991).
7. Merriam-Webster Dictionary, 2013 Internet edition.
8. See http://www.aa.org/en_pdfs/smf-121_en.pdf.

Franciscan Spirituality: Telling the Story

1. I was first exposed to the notion of "story spirituality by Fr. Damian Isabell, OFM, at a pilgrimage workshop in Assisi in 1978. He spells out this notion in Damian Isabell, OFM, *Workbook for Franciscan Sources* (Chicago: Franciscan Herald Press, 1979), pgs. 9–14.
2. "The Mirror of Perfection," #85, in *Francis of Assisi: The Prophet*, volume 3 of *Francis of Assisi: Early Documents* (New York: New City Press), p. 333.
3. See note 2 in Spirituality and Religion.

Who Are You, O God? Who Am I?

1. "The Deeds of Blessed Francis and His Companions" #37, in *Francis of Assisi: The Prophet*, p. 455.
2. Francis of Assisi, "The Praises of God," in *Francis of Assisi: The Saint*, volume 1 of *Francis of Assisi: Early Documents*, etc., p. 109.
3. See note 1 above.
4. Francis of Assisi, "Undated Writings: The Admonitions," XIX, in *The Saint*, p. 135.
5. Ibid., #52, p. 456.

The Big Wow: The Incarnation

1. Thomas of Celano, "The Life of St. Francis," Book 1, #84, in *The Saint*, p. 254.

2. Br. William Short, OFM, *St. Francis of Assisi: A New Way of Being Christian*, Disc 5, Topic 13, Tracks 4–8, Now You Know Media, Inc. 2007.

3. Anselm of Canterbury, *Cur Deus Homo?* Book 2, Chapters VI and VII found in Fordham University Internet History Sourcebooks at http://www.fordham.edu/halsall/basis/anselm-curdeus.asp.

4. Iranaeus of Lyons, "Against Heresies (Book 5, Preface)," in http://www.newadvent.org/fathers/0103500.htm.

5. Francis of Assisi, "The Earlier Rule," Chapter 23, in *The Saint*, pgs. 81–82.

6. Ilia Dilio, OSF, *The Humility of God* (Cincinnati: St. Anthony Messenger Press, 2005), p. 39.

7. See Dilio, OSF. Chapter 2, pgs. 37–49 for a fuller explanation of this thought.

8. Dilio, "Revisiting the Franciscan Doctrine of Christ," in *Theological Studies*, 64, 3, March 1, 2003.

The Cross, Suffering, and Transformation

1. St. Bonaventure, "The Major Legend," Chapter 2, in *Francis of Assisi*, etc., p. 536.

2. For a full account of the *stigmata*, see St. Bonaventure, etc., Chapter 8, pgs. 630–639.

3. Ibid., p. 631–632.
4. Dilio, *Crucified Love* (Quincy, IL: Franciscan Press, 1998), p. 99.
5. Ibid., p. 100.

The Eucharist

1. Francis of Assisi, "A Salutation of the Blessed Virgin Mary," in *The Saint*, p. 163.
2. Francis of Assisi, "A Letter to the Entire Order," in *The Saint*, p. 118.
3. Fr. Dan Crosby, OFM., Cap., *Becoming the Eucharist We Celebrate*, 12 CD series from Now You Know Media, 2012.

The Church

1. Francis of Assisi, "The Later Rule," Chapter 2, in *The Saint*, etc., p. 100.
2. Francis of Assisi, "A Salutation of the Blessed Virgin Mary," in *The Saint*, p. 163.
3. Francis of Assisi, "The Earlier Rule," Chapter 12 in *The Saint*, Pgs. 79–81, also see Bro. William Short, OFM, *A Franciscan Retreat*, Disc 3, Topic 8, Track s11–20 (Now You Know Media, Inc. 2011).

The Spirit of Prayer and Devotion

1. Francis of Assisi, "The Later Rule," Chapter 5 in *The Saint*, p. 102. See also "A Letter to Brother Anthony of Padua," p. 107 of the same volume.
2. Francis of Assisi, "The Earlier Rule," Chapter 23, in *The Saint*, p. 85.

Penance

1. See note 3 in The Cross, Suffering and Transformation.

Poverty

1. Francis of Assisi, "The Later Rule," etc., Chapter 1, in *The Saint*, p. 100.
2. See Johannes Baptist Metz, *Poverty of Spirit*, New York, Paulist Press, 1968, 1998.

Minority—Being Little Among God's Little Ones

1. Celano, "Life of St. Francis," Book 1, Chapter 6, 15, in *The Saint*, p. 193.
2. Ibid., Chapter 7, p. 195.
3. Francis of Assisi, "The Testament," in *The Saint*, p. 124.

Spiritual Nakedness

1. St. Bonaventure, "Major legend of St. Francis," Chapter 15, in *Francis of Assisi: The Founder*, etc. p. 642.

Love of Creation

1. "The Assisi Compilation," *#83*, in *The Founder, p. 186.*
2. See Elizabeth Johnson, *Ask the Beasts: Darwin and the Love of God*, (New York: Bloomsbury, 2014).
3. Pope John Paul II, *Inter Sanctos* (Vatican City, November 29, 1979).
4. Pope Francis, Homily at Inaugural Mass (Vatican City, March 19, 2013).

Brotherhood/Sisterhood

1. Celano, "Life of St. Francis," Book 1, Chapter 8, in *The Saint*, p. 210.
2. Francis of Assisi, "The Testament," in *The Saint*, p. 125.
3. Francis of Assisi, "The Undated Writings, Admonition," IV, in *The Saint*, p. 130.

Always Preaching

1. Francis of Assisi, "The Earlier Rule," Chapter 17, in *Saint*, pgs. 75–76.
2. Francis of Assisi, "The Later Rule," Chapter 9, in *The Saint*, p. 105.

Instruments of Peace

1. St. Bonaventure, "The Major Legend," etc., Chapter 6, p. 100.
2. Ibid., pgs. 602–604.
3. Ibid,.
4. *Legend of Perugia* #44, in *St. Francis of Assisi: Omnibus of Sources*, ed. Marion A., Habig (Chicago: Franciscan Herald Press, 1973).
5. Francis of Assisi, "The Earlier Rule," etc. Chapter 16, in *The Saint*, p. 74.

Conclusion

1. Francis of Assisi, "The Later Rule," etc., Chapter 1, in *The Saint*, p. 100.
2. Pope Francis, *Evangelii Gaudium*, #6, Vatican City, November 24, 2013.

Appendix

I HAVE INCLUDED in this appendix some of the prayers composed by St. Francis that are referred to in this book. I have included as well the story of Francis telling brother Leo what is perfect joy, which I described briefly in the concluding chapter. Rather than using the critical texts of these items found in the three volume *Francis of Assisi: Early Documents*, I have used translations from Internet sites that are easier to read.

Prayer before the Cross at San Damiano

Most High, glorious God,
enlighten the darkness of my heart and give me
true faith, certain hope, and perfect charity,
sense and knowledge, Lord, that I may carry out
Your holy and true command. Amen.

From http://www.shrinesf.org/franciscan-prayer.html

The Praises of God

You are holy Lord God Who does wonderful things.
You are strong. You are great. You are the most high.
You are the almighty king. You holy Father,
King of heaven and earth.
You are three and one, the Lord God of gods;
You are the good, all good, the highest good,
Lord God living and true.
You are love, charity; You are wisdom, You are humility,
You are patience, You are beauty, You are meekness,
You are security, You are rest,
You are gladness and joy, You are our hope, You are justice,
You are moderation, You are all our riches to sufficiency.
You are beauty, You are meekness,
You are the protector, You are our custodian and defender,
You are strength, You are refreshment. You are our hope,
You are our faith, You are our charity,
You are all our sweetness, You are our eternal life:
Great and wonderful Lord, Almighty God, Merciful Savior.

Francis of Assisi, *The Praises of God*, 1224
From http://www.custodia.org/default.asp?id=1453

Canticle of the Creatures

Most High, all-powerful, good Lord,
Yours are the praises, the glory, and the honor, and all blessing,
To You alone, Most High, do they belong,
and no human is worthy to mention Your name.
Praised be You, my Lord, with all Your creatures,
especially Sir Brother Sun,
Who is the day and through whom You give us light.
And he is beautiful and radiant with great splendor;
and bears a likeness of You, Most High One.

Praised be You, my Lord, through Sister Moon and the stars,
in heaven You formed them clear and precious and beautiful.
Praised be You, my Lord, through Brother Wind,
and through the air, cloudy and serene,
and every kind of weather,
through whom You give sustenance to Your creatures.
Praised be You, my Lord, through Sister Water,
who is very useful and humble and precious and chaste.
Praised be You, my Lord, through Brother Fire,
through whom You light the night,
and he is beautiful and playful and robust and strong.
Praised be You, my Lord, through our Sister Mother Earth,
who sustains and governs us,
and who produces various fruit with colored flowers and herbs.

*Praised be You, my Lord, through those
who give pardon for Your love,
and bear infirmity and tribulation.
Blessed are those who endure in peace
for by You, Most High, shall they be crowned.*

*Praised be You, my Lord, through our Sister Bodily Death,
from whom no one living can escape.
Woe to those who die in mortal sin.
Blessed are those whom death will find in Your most holy will,
for the second death shall do them no harm.*

*Praise and bless my Lord and give Him thanks
and serve Him with great humility.*

Francis of Assisi, *Canticle of the Creatures,* 1225
From: http://www.custodia.org/default.asp?id=1454

Perfect Joy

HOW ST FRANCIS, WALKING ONE DAY WITH BROTHER LEO, EXPLAINED TO HIM WHAT THINGS ARE PERFECT JOY

One day in winter, as St Francis was going with Brother Leo from Perugia to St Mary of the Angels, and was suffering greatly from the cold, he called to Brother Leo, who was walking on before him, and said to him: "Brother Leo, if it were to please God that the Friars Minor should give, in all lands, a great example of holiness and edification, write down, and note carefully, that this would not be perfect joy." A little further on, St Francis called to him a second time: "O Brother Leo, if the Friars Minor were to make the lame to walk, if they should make straight the crooked, chase away demons, give sight to the blind, hearing to the deaf, speech to the dumb, and, what is even a far greater work, if they should raise the dead after four days, write that this would not be perfect joy." Shortly after, he cried out again: "O Brother Leo, if the Friars Minor knew all languages; if they were versed in all science; if they could explain all Scripture; if they had the gift of prophecy, and could reveal, not only all future things, but likewise the secrets of all consciences and all souls, write that this would not be perfect joy." After proceeding a few steps farther, he cried out again with a loud voice: "O Brother Leo, thou little lamb of God! if the Friars

Minor could speak with the tongues of angels; if they could explain the course of the stars; if they knew the virtues of all plants; if all the treasures of the earth were revealed to them; if they were acquainted with the various qualities of all birds, of all fish, of all animals, of men, of trees, of stones, of roots, and of waters—write that this would not be perfect joy." Shortly after, he cried out again: "O Brother Leo, if the Friars Minor had the gift of preaching so as to convert all infidels to the faith of Christ, write that this would not be perfect joy." Now when this manner of discourse had lasted for the space of two miles, Brother Leo wondered much within himself; and, questioning the saint, he said: "Father, I pray thee teach me wherein is perfect joy." St Francis answered: "If, when we shall arrive at St Mary of the Angels, all drenched with rain and trembling with cold, all covered with mud and exhausted from hunger; if, when we knock at the convent-gate, the porter should come angrily and ask us who we are; if, after we have told him, `We are two of the brethren', he should answer angrily, `What ye say is not the truth; ye are but two impostors going about to deceive the world, and take away the alms of the poor; begone I say'; if then he refuse to open to us, and leave us outside, exposed to the snow and rain, suffering from cold and hunger till nightfall—then, if we accept such injustice, such cruelty and such contempt with patience, without being ruffled and without murmuring, believing with humility and charity that the porter really knows us, and that it is God who maketh him to speak thus against us, write down, O Brother Leo, that this is perfect joy. And if we knock again, and the porter come out in anger to drive us away with oaths and blows, as if we were vile impostors, saying, `Begone, miserable robbers! to to the hospital, for here you shall neither eat nor sleep!'–and if we accept all this with patience, with joy, and with charity, O Brother Leo, write that this indeed is perfect joy. And if, urged by cold and hunger, we knock again, calling to the porter and entreating him with many tears to open to us and give us shelter, for the love of God, and if he come out more angry than before, exclaiming, `These are but importunate rascals, I will deal with them as they deserve'; and taking a knotted stick, he seize us by the hood, throwing us on the ground, rolling us in the snow, and shall beat and wound us with the knots in the stick–if we bear all these injuries with patience and joy, thinking of the sufferings of our Blessed Lord, which we would share out of love for him, write, O Brother Leo, that here, finally, is perfect joy. And now, brother, listen to the conclusion. Above all the graces and all the gifts of the Holy Spirit which Christ grants to his friends, is the grace of overcoming oneself, and accepting willingly, out of love for Christ, all suffering, injury, discomfort and contempt; for in all other gifts of God we cannot glory, seeing they proceed not from ourselves but from God, according to the words of the Apostle, `What hast thou that thou hast not received from God? and if thou hast received it, why dost thou glory as if thou hadst not received it?' But in the cross of tribulation and affliction we may glory, because, as the Apostle says again, `I will not glory save in the cross of our Lord Jesus Christ.' Amen."

http://www.ewtn.com/library/mary/flowers1.htm

Note: This is somewhat a shortened version of Francis's answer to the question of what is perfect Joy, but it makes for easier reading than the full text cited earlier in this book.

Bibliography

In this bibliography, I have included several works that may be helpful to the reader but which are not referenced in this book. I have divided these works into categories.

I.   Additional Source Books.

> *Francis and Clare: The Complete Works.* Translated by Regis Armstrong, OFM, and Ignatius Brady, OFM, from *Classics of Western Spirituality.* New York: Paulist Press, 1982.

> *Bonaventure: The Soul's Journey into God, The Tree of Life, The Life of St. Francis (Classics of Western Spirituality).* Translated with introduction by Ewert Cousins. New York: Paulist Press, 1978.

II. Lives of St. Francis

Chesterton, Gilbert Keith. *Saint Francis of Assisi.* Peabody, MA: Hendrickson Publishers, 2008 (This is an updated edition of the work originally published by Chesterton in 1957.) This is a well done and easily readable life of Francis.

Fortini, Arnaldo. *Francis of Assisi.* Translated by Helen Moak. New York: Crossroad, 1981. I would recommend this life of Francis for those interested in the history and culture of his times. It is for those looking for good research and scholarship around Francis.

Spoto, Donald. *Reluctant Saint: The Life of Francis of Assisi.* New York: Viking Compass, 2002.

Vaucher, Andre. *Francis of Assisi: The Life and Afterlife of a Medieval Saint.* Translated by Michael F. Cusato. New Haven: Yale University Press, 2012. Vaucher not only tells of the Life of Francis but notes his influence that of his order on the Church through the years.

III. Franciscan Meditations

These works by Murray Bodo, OFM, provide nice ongoing reflections on Francis and Franciscan spirituality.

Bodo, Murray, OFM. *Francis: the Journey and the Dream.* Cincinnati: St. Anthony Messenger Press, 1972.

Bodo, Murray, OFM. *Through the Year with Francis of Assisi.* New York: Image Books, 1987.

Bodo, Murray, OFM. *Tales of St. Francis: Ancient Stories for Contemporary Living.* New York: Doubleday, 1988.

IV. Works on St. Clare.

I must admit that one shortcoming of this book has been the lack of mention of St. Clare. Here are two fine works on this great woman and friend of St. Francis, one older and one more recent.

De Robeck, Nesta. *St. Clare of Assisi.* Chicago: Franciscan Herald Press, 1980. Reprinted with permission of Bruce Publishing Company of Milwaukee, originally printed in 1951.

Carney, Margaret, OSF. *The First Franciscan Woman and Her Form of Life.* Quincy, IL: Franciscan Press, 1993.

V. Books about St. Francis and Franciscan Spirituality.

These fine works by different authors offer various perspectives on Franciscan spirituality.

Doyle, Eric, OFM. *St. Francis and the Song of the Brotherhood.* New York: Seabury Press, 1981.

Carretto, Carlo. *I, Francis.* Translated from Italian by Robert R. Barr. Maryknoll, NY: Orbis Books, 1982.

Moses, Paul. *The Saint and the Sultan:The Crusades, Islam and Francis of Assisi's Mission of Peace.* New York: Doubleday, 2009.

VI. Books presenting the thought of Scotus and Bonaventure for Contemporary thinkers.

There are two fine books by Sr. Ilia Dilio, OSF, referenced in the endnotes. I would also suggest looking at her works on creation, which offer a Franciscan perspective on this important contemporary issue.

Dilio, Ilia, OSF. *Christ in Evolution.* Maryknoll, NY: Orbis Books, 2008.

Dilio, Ilia, OSF. Keith Douglas, OFM, and Pamela Wood. *Care for Creation: A Franciscan Spirituality of Creation.* Cincinnati: St. Anthony Messenger Press, 2008.

Ingam, Mary Beth. *Scotus for Dunces.* St. Bonaventure, NY: The Franciscan Institute, 2003.

Horan, Dan, OFM. *Dating God, Live and Love in the Way of St. Francis.* Cincinnati: St. Anthony Messenger Press, 2012.

In this book Father Dan presents in a very clear way how the vision of Francis and his followers, Bonaventure and Scotus can shape our spiritual journey today.